YEAR 7

NUMERACY

NAPLAN*-FORMAT PRACTICE TESTS
with answers

Essential preparation for Year 7
NAPLAN* Tests in Numeracy

DON ROBENS

CORONEOS PUBLICATIONS

* These tests have been produced by Coroneos Publications independently of Australian
  governments and are not officially endorsed publications of the NAPLAN program

YEAR 7 NUMERACY
NAPLAN*-FORMAT PRACTICE TESTS with answers
© Don Robens 2010
First published by Coroneos Publications 2010. Revised 2014.

ISBN 978-1-921565-54-0

* These tests have been produced by Coroneos Publications independently of Australian governments and are not officially endorsed publications of the NAPLAN program

This book is available from recognised booksellers or contact:

Coroneos Publications

Telephone: (02) 9838 9265   **Facsimile:** (02) 9838 8982
Business Address: 2/195 Prospect Highway Seven Hills 2147
Website: www.coroneos.com.au
E-mail: info@fivesenseseducation.com.au

2024.03.28

Contents

NOTE:

- Students have 40 minutes to complete a test. (80 mins for both tests)

- Students must use 2B or HB pencils only.

1   2.75, 3.50, 4.25, 5.0 …

Shade one bubble

What is the rule to continue this decimal number pattern?

○ increase by 0.25

○ increase by 0.75

○ decrease by 0.25

○ increase by 0.55

---

2   This road post shows the water depth in a flood.

Approximately how deep is the water?

○ 55 metres

○ 5.05 metres

○ 5.5 metres

○ 5.5 centimetres

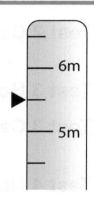

— 6m

— 5m

---

3   Which of these has the same value as 14 × 6?

○ 10 × 4 + 4 × 6

○ 10 × 6 + 4 × 6

○ 10 × 24

○ 14 × 6 + 4

---

4   A regular pentagon is cut in half.

What is the shape of each half?

○ rectangle

○ pentagon

○ quadrilateral

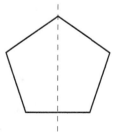

---

5   **Which shows an obtuse angle?**

Shade one bubble

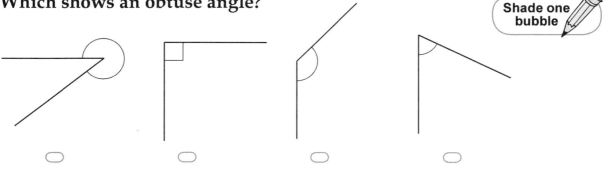

◯   ◯   ◯   ◯

6   **Which has the *least* liquid in it?**

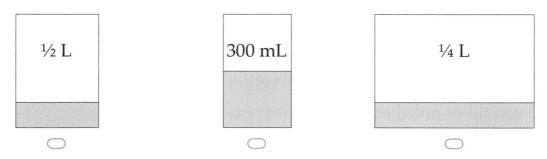

| ½ L | 300 mL | ¼ L |

◯   ◯   ◯

7   A number is multiplied by itself and then 7 is added.

The answer is 16.

What is the number? _____

8   The area of this shaded rectangle is 84 cm².

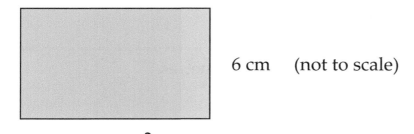

6 cm   (not to scale)

_____ ?

What is the length of the rectangle? _____ cm

9 Bricks make this pattern.

If this pattern continues, how many bricks will be in the 6th row?

23	27	21	20
○	○	○	○

10 A container holds 12 red, 9 blue, 11 yellow and 22 green marbles.

A person takes one marble from the container.

What is the chance that the marble is blue?

½	⅓	¼	⅙
○	○	○	○

11 Jim has 28 green grapes and 14 purple grapes.

What fraction of the grapes is purple?

½	⅓	¼	⅙
○	○	○	○

12 A rectangular paddock has a perimeter of 46 metres.

The length of the longer side is 18 metres.

What is length of the shorter side?

_____ metres.

13 What is $20 as a percentage of $100?

Shade one bubble

25%	50%	30%	20%
○	○	○	○

14 A balance shows that 3 cans have the same mass as 1 block.

How many blocks balance 2 blocks and 6 cans?

6	4	5	8
○	○	○	○

15 A pile of papers has 999 sheets.

One-third of the sheets are blue and the rest are white.

50% of the white sheets are used.

How many sheets are used?

300	350	334	333
○	○	○	○

16 The number of shapes in groups is shown below.

Number of groups	2	3	4	5
Number of shapes	8	12	16	20

What is the minimum number of groups needed for 32 shapes?

6	7	8	9
○	○	○	○

17 A 3D object has 5 faces. Only 2 faces are triangles.

The other 3 are rectangles.

The object is a

prism	pyramid	cube	triangle
○	○	○	○

18 Wendy cut 2 corners off a rectangular prism.

How many edges does the object now have?

_____ edges

19 The time difference between London and Sydney on the same day is shown below.

Shade one bubble

London 9:15 a.m.	Sydney 7:15 p.m.

When it is 4:30 p.m. on Wednesday in London, what time is it in Sydney?

○ 3:30 a.m. Wednesday

○ 2:30 a.m. Tuesday

○ 4:30 a.m. Wednesday

○ 2:30 a.m. Thursday

20 **Which arrow is pointing to the location of ¾ on this number line?**

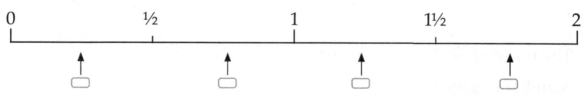

21 △ and □ are numbers. □ and △ are related by a rule.

□	△
2	15
3	25
4	35
5	45

What is the rule?

○ $\triangle = 10 \times \square - 5$

○ $\triangle = 12 \times \square - 10$

○ $\triangle = 15 \times \square + 3$

22 What fraction is halfway between ⅝ and ⁶⁄₈?

_____

23 The temperature at the base of a mountain is 12°C.

The temperature at the top is 25°C colder than the base.

What is temperature at the top?   _____°C

24 The dimensions of a large room are double the dimensions
of a small room. Both rooms are rectangular prisms.
The volume of the small room is 12 cubic metres.

What is the volume of the large room?

○ 80 cubic metres

○ 76 cubic metres

○ 96 cubic metres

○ 90 cubic metres

25 **Which set of fractions is ordered from smallest to largest?**

○ ½, ¾, ⅔, ⁸⁄₁₂

○ ½, ¾, ⁸⁄₁₀, ¹²⁄₁₂

○ ½, ⅝, ⁷⁄₁₂, ⁸⁄₂₀

○ ⅔, ⅓, ⁶⁄₈, ¹²⁄₂₀

26 A clock shows 4 o'clock.

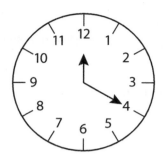

What is the size of the smaller angle between the minute and the hour hands?

_____

27

| 16:30 |

Shade one bubble

What analog time is the same as the above 24 hour time?

2:30 a.m.   4:30 p.m.   6:30 p.m.   4:30 a.m.

◯   ◯   ◯   ◯

28 Another way of writing 7^2 is

◯ 7 + 7

◯ 7 × 7

◯ 7 × 2

◯ 7 + 7 + 7 + 7

29 A face of a prism has been glued to the same size base of a triangular-based pyramid.

How many faces does the new shape have? _____

30 What is $20 as a percentage of $80?

Shade one bubble

20%	25%	30%	15%
○	○	○	○

31 Which fraction has the same value as 3¼?

¹²⁄₄	¹⁴⁄₄	¹⁵⁄₄	¹³⁄₄
○	○	○	○

32 This picture shows the position of three bus stops on the road leading to a school. Bus stop B is exactly halfway between bus stop A and bus stop C. (not to scale)

School · · · · · · · · · · · · Bus Stop A · · · Bus Stop B · · · Bus Stop C

1.5 km

3.2 km

What is the distance between the school and bus stop B? _____ km

Shade one
bubble

1 $\square = 3$

$\triangle = 4$

$\bigcirc + \square = \triangle + \triangle$

Which number does $\bigcirc$ equal?

2	5	4	6
⬭	⬭	⬭	⬭

2   In 1914, World War 1 began.

In 2010, how long is it since World War 1 began?

94 years	95 years	96 years	196 years
⬭	⬭	⬭	⬭

3   Grahame travelled 135 kilometres in 3 hours.

What was his average speed in kilometres per hour?

40	45	50	55
⬭	⬭	⬭	⬭

4   Two places are 3.7 cm apart on a map.

On a map 1 cm represents 5 km.

What is the actual distance between the two places?

1.65 km	1.84 km	18.5 km	185 km
⬭	⬭	⬭	⬭

5   **Round 9 508 659 km to the nearest thousand kilometres.**

9 508 000	9 509 000	9 6000 000	9 507 000
⬭	⬭	⬭	⬭

6

-3   -2   -1   0   1

The arrow points to a position on the number line.

What number is at this point? _____

7   Sarah wrote a number on a piece a paper.

If she multiplied her number by 6 and then divided by 3, the answer is 28.

What is the number? _____

8   There are 3 properties for sale.

Which is the largest property?

Shade one bubble

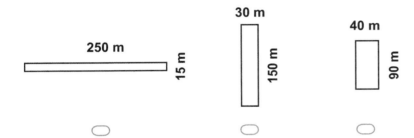

250 m   15 m

30 m   150 m

40 m   90 m

   ⬯   ⬯   ⬯

9   A water tank has a capacity of 9.50 kilolitres.

How many litres does the water tank hold when it is full?

9 500   950   95.00   950.0

  ⬯   ⬯   ⬯   ⬯

10 $6.56 + 4.86 =$ _____ $+ 2.60$

11   Alan bought 3 pens (all the same price) and a $3 exercise book. The cost was $12.60.

Shade one bubble

What would 2 pens and a $2 exercise book cost?

$8.60 $8.20 $8.80 $8.40

  ⬯   ⬯   ⬯   ⬯

12 $45 \times$ _____ $= 15$

What is the value of _____?

⅔   ½   ⅓   ⅖
○   ○   ○   ○

---

13 Jack bought a tent. Its price was 15% less than its original price.

The original price was $250.

What did Jack pay for the tent?

$215 $220 $212.50 $215.50
○   ○   ○   ○

---

14 A book has 24 pages.

8 pages had illustrations.

What fraction of the book is illustrated?

½   ¼   ⅓   ⅔
○   ○   ○   ○

---

15 A person sets their watch and alarm clock to different times.

Watch	7:30 (a.m.)
Alarm clock	**10 past 8 o'clock (a.m.)**

When the alarm clock shows 5 past 10 o'clock a.m. what time will their watch show?

9:30 a.m.   10:45 a.m.   9:25 a.m.   10:25 a.m.
○   ○   ○   ○

16 The time is 08:25.

What time will it be in 48 minutes?

_____ : _____

---

17 The height of one brick is about 8 cm.

About how high would 250 bricks be in centimetres?

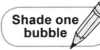

Shade one bubble

| 1 500 | 2 500 | 2 000 | 1 750 |

◯   ◯   ◯   ◯

---

18 This calculation gives the average speed (kilometres per hour) of a rocket.

$$\frac{52.525 - 7.655}{0.02}$$

What is the average speed of the rocket?

_____ kilometres per hour

---

19 The mean (average) of four numbers is 36.

A fifth number is added and the mean becomes 38.

The number that was added was

Shade one bubble

| 45 | 46 | 36 | 56 |

◯   ◯   ◯   ◯

---

20 A person used identical cubes to build a rectangular prism.

There were 15 cubes in its base.

90 cubes were used altogether.

Which of these could be the dimensions of the prism?

| 10 × 4 × 2 | 5 × 3 × 6 | 6 × 4 × 8 | 12 × 2 × 4 |

◯   ◯   ◯   ◯

---

21 An orchardist has 3 times as many apple trees as plum trees. Altogether there are 60 trees.

How many apple trees are there? _____

22 Which of these is in ascending order?

Shade one bubble

- ○ 0.02,   0.2,   0.002,   0.01
- ○ 0.004,   0.04,   0.40,   0.44
- ○ 0.03,   0.3,   0.005,   0.006
- ○ 1.0,   1.02,   1.005,   1.55

23 A pyramid has a square base. The area of the square base is 44 100 m².

What is the length of one side of the base? _____ m

24 Which number is eight thousand and twenty-three?

Shade one bubble

8 203	8 033	8 023	8203
○	○	○	○

25 Which number is exactly halfway between 1¼ and 2¾?

1 ½	2 ¼	2	1 ¾
○	○	○	○

26 Ruth ran for 30 seconds. She moved at a speed of 8 metres a second.

How far did she go?

50m	250m	260m	240m
○	○	○	○

27 A car uses an average of 7 litres of fuel for every 100 km travelled.

How many litres would the car use to travel 350km?

_____ litres

28 One-fifth of the length of Sam's fishing line is 70 cm.

How long is the fishing line? _____ cm

29 A school has 270 students.

90 of the students are in the school hall.

Shade one bubble

The fraction of students in the hall is closest to

one-eighth   one-third   one-quarter   one-half
⬭   ⬭   ⬭   ⬭

30 Peter paid $1.25 for bananas.

Bananas   1 kg for $2.50

How many grams of bananas did he buy?

0.500 g   700 g   500 g   750 g
⬭   ⬭   ⬭   ⬭

31 **How long is there between 3:17 a.m. and 2:10 p.m. on the same day?**

⬭ 10 hours and 35 minutes

⬭ 10 hours and 53 minutes

⬭ 11 hours and 35 minutes

⬭ 10 hours and 43 minutes

32 An electricity bill was $240. The next bill was $180.

What percentage decrease is this?

25%   30%   40%   55%
⬭   ⬭   ⬭   ⬭

1 3.75, 4.25, 4.75 …

Shade one bubble

What is the rule to continue this decimal number pattern?

○ increase by 0.50

○ increase by 0.05

○ decrease by 0.25

○ increase by 0.55

2 This road post shows the water depth in a flood.

Approximately how deep is the water?

○ 6.05 metres

○ 6.25 metres

○ 6.5 metres

○ 6.75 centimetres

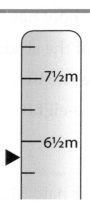

3 **Which of these has the same value as 15 × 7?**

10 × 7 + 5 × 7	10 × 5 + 5 × 7	5 × 35	15 × 6 + 7
○	○	○	○

4 A regular octagon is cut in half.

What is the shape of each half?

○ octagon

○ hexagon

○ quadrilateral

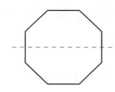

5   **Which shows a reflex angle?**

Shade one bubble

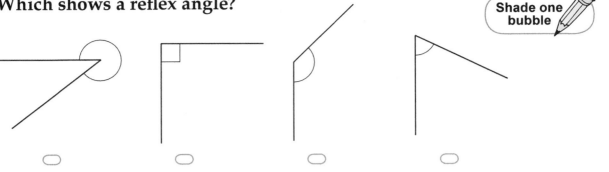

    ◯   ◯   ◯   ◯

6   **Which has the _least_ liquid in it?**

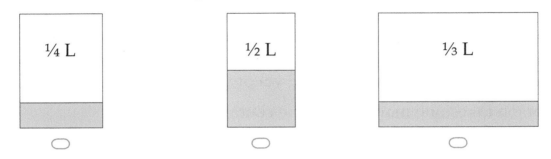

¼ L   ½ L   ⅓ L

    ◯   ◯   ◯

7   A number is multiplied by itself and then 11 is added.

The answer is 75.

What is the number? _____

8   The area of this shaded rectangle is 64 cm^2.

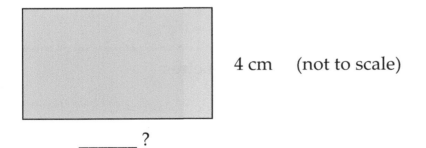

4 cm   (not to scale)

_____ ?

What is the length of the rectangle? _____ cm

9   Bricks make this pattern.

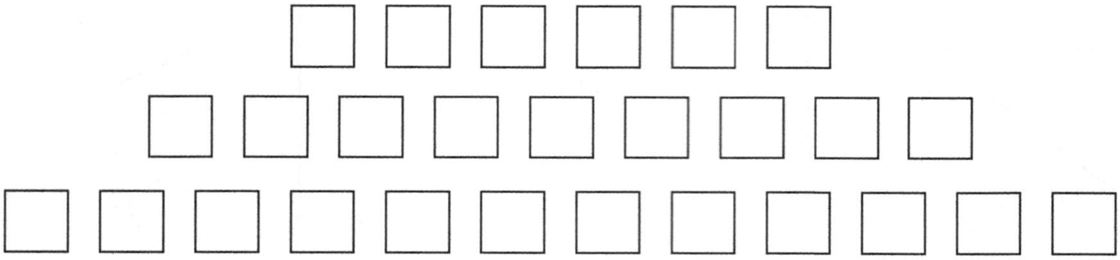

Shade one bubble

If this pattern continues, how many bricks will be in the 9th row?

36   27   30   40

○   ○   ○   ○

10   A container holds 15 red, 6 black, 8 yellow and 25 green marbles.

A person takes one marble from the container.

What is the chance that the marble is black?

½   ⅑   ⅛   ⅙

○   ○   ○   ○

11   Jim has 26 green grapes and 13 purple grapes.

What fraction of the grapes is purple?

½   ⅓   ¼   ⅙

○   ○   ○   ○

12   A rectangular paddock has a perimeter of 34 metres.

The length of the longer side is 9 metres.

What is length of the shorter side?

_____ metres.

13 **What is $40 as a percentage of $100?**

Shade one bubble

45%   4%   40%   44%

○   ○   ○   ○

14 A balance shows that 2 cans have the same mass as 1 block.

How many blocks balance 5 blocks and 6 cans?

6   8   10   12

○   ○   ○   ○

15 A pile of papers has 369 sheets.

One-third of the sheets are blue and the rest are white.

50% of the white sheets are used.

How many sheets are used?

150   120   123   125

○   ○   ○   ○

16 The number of shapes in groups is shown below.

Number of groups	2	3	4	5
Number of shapes	8	12	16	20

What is the minimum number of groups needed for 32 shapes?

6   7   8   9

○   ○   ○   ○

17 A 3D object has 5 faces. 1 face is a square. The other 4 are triangles.

The object is a

prism   pyramid   cube   triangle

○   ○   ○   ○

18 Wendy cut 2 corners off a cube.

How many edges does the object now have?

_____ edges

19 The time difference between City A and City B
on the same day is shown below.

City A 6:15 a.m.	City B 8:15 p.m.

When it is 1:30 p.m. on Sunday in City A, what time is it in City B?

○ 4:30 a.m. Monday

○ 4:00 a.m. Tuesday

○ 3:30 a.m. Monday

○ 4:15 a.m. Thursday

20 Which arrow is pointing to the location of 75% of this number line?

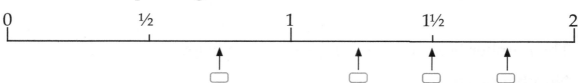

21 △ and □ are numbers. □ and △ are related by a rule.

□	△
2	12
3	18
4	24
5	30

What is the rule?

○ △ = 7 × □ + 1

○ △ = 5 × □ + 2

○ △ = 6 × □ + 0

22 **What fraction is halfway between ¼ and ⁶⁄₈?**

_____

23 The temperature at the base of a mountain is 9°C.

The temperature at the top is 15°C colder than the base.

What is temperature at the top?   _____°C

24 The dimensions of a large room are double those

of a small room. Both rooms are rectangular prisms.

The volume of the small room is 18 cubic metres.

Shade one bubble

What is the volume of the large room?

○ 120 cubic metres

○ 144 cubic metres

○ 150 cubic metres

○ 146 cubic metres

25 **Which set of fractions is ordered from smallest to largest?**

○ ½,   ⅓,   ¼,   ⁶⁄₁₀

○ ¼,   ⅓,   ½,   ¾

○ ⅕,   ⅗,   ½,   ¾

○ ⅕,   ¼,   ½,   ⅓

26 A clock shows 8 o'clock.

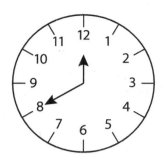

What is the size of the smaller angle between the minute and the hour hands?

_____ °

27

| 14:50 |

Shade one bubble

What analog time is the same as the above 24 hour time?

1:50 p.m.   2:30 p.m.   2:50 p.m.   3:50 p.m.

  ○   ○   ○   ○

28 Another way of writing 9^2 is

○ $9 + 9$

○ 9×1

○ 9×9

○ 9×2

29 A rectangular-based pyramid and a rectangular prism
have been glued together at the base of rectangular-based pyramid.

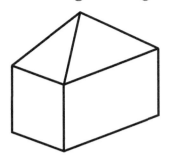

How many faces does the new shape have? _____

30 What is $30 as a percentage of $50?

50%	55%	60%	65%
◯	◯	◯	◯

31 What is the missing number?

6 × _____ = 14 × 3

32 Which fraction has the same value as 4 ¼?

$\frac{9}{4}$	$\frac{16}{4}$	$\frac{15}{4}$	$\frac{17}{4}$
◯	◯	◯	◯

1   □ = 19

△ = 18

○ + □ = △ + △

Which number does ○ equal?

16	17	18	19
○	○	○	○

2   Australian Parliament has been meeting in Canberra since 1927.

In 2010 how many years ago was this?

74 years	73 years	83 years	82 years
○	○	○	○

3   Geoff travelled 168 kilometres in 3 hours.

What was his average speed in kilometres per hour?

46	65	55	56
○	○	○	○

4   Two places are 4.3 cm apart on a map.

On a map 1 cm represents 20 km.

What is the actual distance between the two places?

86 km	85.4 km	21.5 km	85 km
○	○	○	○

5   **Round 7 505 457 km to the nearest ten thousand kilometres.**

7 510 000	7 500 000	7 505 000	7 105 000
○	○	○	○

6   -3   -2   -1   0   1

The arrow points to a position on the number line.

What number is at this point? _____

7   Sarah wrote a number on a piece a paper.

If she multiplied her number by 7 and divided it by 5, the answer is 49.

What is the number? _____

8   There are 3 properties for sale.

Which is the *largest* property?

100 m / 35 m

80 m / 50 m

45 m / 90 m

○   ○   ○

9   A water tank has a capacity of 12.50 kilolitres.

How many litres does the water tank hold when it is full?

12 500   10 250   12.500   1250.00

○   ○   ○   ○

10 7.57 + 4.89 = _____ + 2.80

11 Anne bought 3 pens (all the same price) and an $18 book. They cost $39.

What do 2 pens and a $25 book cost?

$39 $40 $38 $42

○   ○   ○   ○

12 $84 \times$ _____ $= 28$

Shade one
bubble

What is the value of _____?

⅔	½	⅓	⅖
○	○	○	○

---

13 James bought a tent. Its price was 30% less than its original price.

The original price was $350.

What did he pay for the tent?

$215	$245	$250	$240
○	○	○	○

---

14 A book has 28 pages.

7 pages had illustrations.

What fraction of the book is illustrated?

½	¼	⅓	⅔
○	○	○	○

---

15 A person sets their watch and alarm clock to different times.

Watch	6:30 (a.m.)
Alarm clock	**25 past 7 o'clock (a.m.)**

When the alarm clock shows 20 past 2 o'clock (p.m.) what time will their watch show?

1:30 p.m.	1:25 p.m.	1:35 p.m.	2:25 p.m.
○	○	○	○

16 The time is 07:35.

What time will it be in 78 minutes?

_____ : _____

17 The height of one brick is about 14 cm.

About how high would 300 bricks be in centimetres?

Shade one bubble

5 500	4 500	4 000	4 200
⬭	⬭	⬭	⬭

18 This calculation gives the average speed (kilometres per hour) of a space craft over a short time interval.

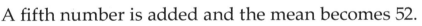

$$\frac{48.565 - 9.640}{0.06}$$

What is the average speed of the space craft?

_____ kilometres per hour

19 The mean (average) of four numbers is 48.

A fifth number is added and the mean becomes 52.

The number that was added was

Shade one bubble

65	68	86	78
⬭	⬭	⬭	⬭

20 A person used identical cubes to build a rectangular prism. There were 28 cubes in its base.

112 cubes were used altogether.

Which of these could be the dimensions of the prism?

7 × 4 × 2	8 × 3 × 4	7 × 4 × 4	4 × 7 × 5
⬭	⬭	⬭	⬭

21 An orchardist has 7 times as many apple trees as other trees. Altogether there are 464 trees.

How many apple trees are there? _____

22 Which of these is in ascending order?

○ 0.028, 0.8, 0.008, 0.09

○ 0.007 0.07 0.70, 7.00

○ 0.01 0.1 0.001 0.001

○ 2.0 2.02 4.005 3.55

23 A pyramid has a square base.

The area of the square base is 3 136 m².

What is the length of one side of the base? _____ m

24 Which number is nine thousand and twenty-three?

9 003	9 023	9 223	9 923
○	○	○	○

25 Which number is exactly halfway between 1¼ and 2½?

1½	1⅘	1⅞	1¾
○	○	○	○

26 Tom ran for 30 seconds. He ran at a speed of 9 metres a second.

How far did he go?

250m	240m	270m	360m
○	○	○	○

27 A car uses an average of 6 litres of fuel for every 100 km travelled.

How many litres would the car use to travel 250km?

_____ litres

---

28 One-sixth of the length of Joe's fishing line is 90 cm.

How long is the fishing line? _____ cm

---

29 A school has 480 students.

120 of the students are in the school hall.

Shade one bubble

The fraction of students who are in the hall is closest to

one-eighth	one-third	one-quarter	one-half
◯	◯	◯	◯

---

30 Peter paid $1.00 for bananas.

Bananas 1 kg for $2.50

How many grams of bananas did he buy?

0.400g	450g	1400g	400g
◯	◯	◯	◯

---

31 How long is there between 5:17 a.m. and 1:30 p.m. on the same day?

◯ 8 hours and 13 minutes

◯ 8 hours and 12 minutes

◯ 9 hours and 13 minutes

◯ 9 hours and 12 minutes

---

32 A person's electricity bill was $240 last time. The next bill it was $180.

What percentage decrease is this?

25%	30%	20%	35%
◯	◯	◯	◯

1   4.05, 3.10, 2.15, 1.20 …

What is the rule to continue this decimal number pattern?

○ increase by 1.20

○ decrease by 0.85

○ decrease by 0.95

○ decrease by 1.05

2   This road post shows the water depth in a flood.

Approximately how deep is the water?

○ 5.05 metres

○ 5.25 metres

○ 5.00 metres

○ 5.75 centimetres

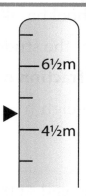

3   **Which of these has the same value as 28 × 6?**

$20 \times 6 + 6 + 8$	$20 \times 6 + 8 \times 6$	6×82	$28 \times 6 + 2$
○	○	○	○

4   **$5¾ is equal to**

$5.20	$5.25	530 c	575 c
○	○	○	○

5 **Which shows 270°?**

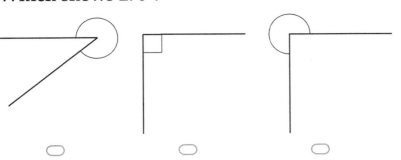

     ⬭   ⬭   ⬭

6 **Which has the *least* liquid in it?**

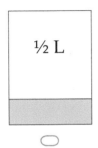   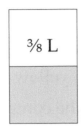   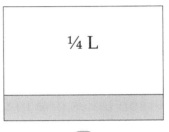

½ L   ⅜ L   ¼ L

     ⬭   ⬭   ⬭

7 A number is multiplied by itself and then 18 is added.

The answer is 274.

What is the number? _____

8 The area of this shaded rectangle is 126 cm².

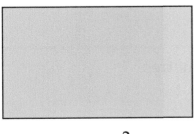

7 cm   (not to scale)

_____ ?

What is the length of the rectangle? _____ cm

9   Blocks make this pattern.

Shade one bubble

If this pattern continues, how many blocks will be in the 11th row?

65   45   55   50

○   ○   ○   ○

10   A container holds 30 red, 9 blue, 5 yellow and 16 green marbles.

A person takes one marble from the container.

What is the chance that the marble is yellow?

½   ¹⁄₁₂   ³⁄₁₀   ¹⁄₁₆

○   ○   ○   ○

11   Jim has 36 green pencils and 9 red pencils.

What fraction of the pencils is red?

½   ⅓   ¼   ⅕

○   ○   ○   ○

12   A rectangular paddock has a perimeter of 38 metres.

The length of the longer side is 14 metres.

What is length of the shorter side?

_____ metres.

13 **What is $25 as a percentage of $25?**

Shade one bubble

95%   100%   80%   85%

◯   ◯   ◯   ◯

14 A balance shows that 5 cans have the same mass as 10 blocks.

How many blocks balance 3 blocks and 3 cans?

6   7   8   9

◯   ◯   ◯   ◯

15 A pile of papers has 420 sheets.

One-third of the sheets are yellow and the rest are white.

50% of the white sheets are used.

How many sheets are used?

145   150   140   165

◯   ◯   ◯   ◯

16 The number of shapes in groups is shown below.

Number of groups	2	3	4	5
Number of shapes	4	16	28	30

What is the minimum number of groups needed for 72 shapes?

6   7   8   9

◯   ◯   ◯   ◯

17 A 3D object has no faces, vertices or edges.

The object is a

prism   pyramid   cube   sphere

◯   ◯   ◯   ◯

18 **0.250 of $12 is**

Shade one
bubble

$6 $3 $4 $5

○   ○   ○   ○

---

19 The time difference between City A and City B on the same day is shown below.

City A 12:25 a.m.	City B 1:45 p.m.

When it is 4:30 p.m. on Friday in City A, what time is it in City B?

○ 4:30 a.m. Friday

○ 4:00 a.m. Saturday

○ 5:50 a.m. Saturday

○ 4:50 a.m. Friday

---

20 Which arrow is pointing to the location of 100% of this number line?

0   ½   1   1½   2

⬆   ⬆   ⬆   ⬆
○   ○   ○   ○

---

21 △ and □ are numbers. □ and △ are related by a rule.

□	△
2	14
3	21
4	28
5	35

What is the rule?

○ △ = 5 × □ + 1

○ △ = 6 × □ + 2

○ △ = 7 × □ + 0

22 **What fraction is halfway between 1/4 and 8/8?**

____

23 The temperature of some water is 14°C.

The water temperature becomes 19°C colder.

What is temperature of the water now? __________°C

24 The dimensions of a large room are triple those of a small room. Both rooms are rectangular prisms.

Shade one bubble

The volume of the small room is 10 cubic metres.

What is the volume of the large room?

- ⬭ 280 cubic metres
- ⬭ 275 cubic metres
- ⬭ 270 cubic metres
- ⬭ 250 cubic metres

25 **Which set of fractions is ordered from smallest to largest?**

- ⬭ 1/2 1/8 1/4 3/10
- ⬭ 1/4 2/3 1/2 5/4
- ⬭ 1/5 3/5 7/10 4/5
- ⬭ 1/5 4/5 1/2 1

26 A clock shows 1 o'clock.

Shade one bubble

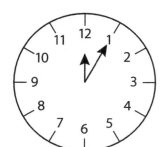

What is the size of the larger angle between the minute and the hour hands?

_____ °

27

19:40

What analog time is the same as the above 24 hour time?

7:50 a.m.   7:40 p.m.   7:40 a.m.   8:50 p.m.
○   ○   ○   ○

28 Another way of writing 7³ is

$7 + 7 + 7$ 7×3 $7 \times 7 \times 7$ 70×3
○   ○   ○   ○

29 19.5 km is equal to
○ 195 m
○ 1 950 m
○ 19 500 m
○ 1.95 m

30 What is $37.50 as a percentage of $100?

Shade one bubble

37.00%   37.55 %   37.50%   37.05%

◯   ◯   ◯   ◯

---

31 What is the missing number?

14 × _____ = 16 × 7

---

32 Which fraction has the same value as 9 ¼?

$\frac{38}{4}$ $\frac{39}{4}$ $\frac{33}{4}$ $\frac{37}{4}$

◯   ◯   ◯   ◯

Shade one bubble

1   □ = 19

△ = 16

○ + □ = △ + △ + △

Which number does ○ equal?

16	17	18	29
○	○	○	○

2   A road was completed in 1893.

In 2010, how many years ago was this?

114 years	117 years	179 years	217 years
○	○	○	○

3   A plane travelled 1 076 kilometres in 4 hours.

What was the average speed in kilometres per hour?

289	267	259	269
○	○	○	○

4   Two places are 7.8 cm apart on a map.

On a map 1 cm represents 15 km.

What is the actual distance between the two places?

116 km	117 km	117.5 km	171 km
○	○	○	○

5   **Round 3 852 487 kL to the nearest hundred thousand kilolitres.**

3 060 000	3 900 000	3 800 000	3 905 000
○	○	○	○

6

-3   -2   -1   0   1

The arrow points to a position on the number line.

What number is at this point? _____

7   Sarah wrote a number on a piece a paper.

If she multiplied her number by 7 and divided it by 7, the answer is 80.

What is the number? _____

8   There are 3 properties for sale.

Which is the *smallest* property?

Shade one bubble

90 m
35 m

45 m
80 m

65 m
70 m

○   ○   ○

9   A water tank has a capacity of 19.50 kilolitres.

How many litres does the water tank hold when it is full?

19 500   1 950   1 905.50   195.00

○   ○   ○   ○

10   18.97 + 7.89 = _____ + 2.57

11   Alan bought 6 pens (all the same price) and an $18 book.

These cost $84.

Shade one bubble

What do 2 pens and a $29 book cost?

$39 $40 $51 $42

○   ○   ○   ○

12 $92 \times \underline{\hspace{1cm}} = 46$

Shade one
bubble

What is the value of _____?

⅔   ½   ⅓   ⅖

○   ○   ○   ○

---

13 Grace bought a car. Its price was 35% less than its original price.

The original price was $14 500.

What did she pay for the car?

$9 215 $9 425 $9 250 $9 240

○   ○   ○   ○

---

14 A book has 96 pages.

64 pages had illustrations.

What fraction of the book is illustrated?

½   ¼   ⅓   ⅔

○   ○   ○   ○

---

15 A person sets their watch and alarm clock to different times.

Watch	00:45 (a.m.)
Alarm clock	**35 past 5 o'clock (a.m.)**

When the alarm clock shows 10 to 6 o'clock (p.m.) what time
will their watch show?

1:10 p.m.   1:00 p.m.   1:15 p.m.   12:00 p.m.

○   ○   ○   ○

16   The time is 23:35.

What time will it be in 58 minutes?

_____ : _____

---

17   The height of one brick is about 17 cm.

About how high would 450 bricks be in centimetres?

Shade one bubble

7 650	6 650	7 560	7 750
◯	◯	◯	◯

---

18   This calculation gives the average speed (kilometres per hour) of a space craft over a short time interval.

$$\frac{38.965 - 7.670}{2.09}$$

What is the average speed of the space craft?

_____ kilometres per hour

---

19   The mean (average) of six numbers is 87.

A seventh number is added and the mean becomes 90.

Shade one bubble

The number that was added was

105	108	118	128
◯	◯	◯	◯

---

20   A person used identical cubes to build a rectangular prism.

There were 36 cubes in its base.

252 cubes were used altogether.

Which of these could be the dimensions of the prism?

$9 \times 4 \times 6$	$4 \times 9 \times 8$	$9 \times 4 \times 7$	$4 \times 9 + 7$
◯	◯	◯	◯

21 A car dealer has 8 times as many new cars as used cars.

Altogether there are 816 cars.

How many new cars are there? _____

Shade one bubble

22 Which of these is in ascending order?

- ⃝ 0.08 0.008 0.88 0.0008
- ⃝ 0.004 0.04 0.40 4.40
- ⃝ 0.006 0.06 0.6 0.66
- ⃝ 3.5 3.05 3.005 30.5

23 A pyramid has a square base.

The area of the square base is 1 225 m².

What is the length of one side of the base? _____ m

24 Which number is seven thousand, two hundred and two?

Shade one bubble

7 002	7 022	7 202	7 222
⃝	⃝	⃝	⃝

25 Which number is exactly halfway between 1¾ and 2½?

2 ¼	2 ⅛	2	2 ⅓
⃝	⃝	⃝	⃝

26 Tim ran for 1 ½ minutes. He ran at a speed of 8 metres a second.

How far did he go?

802 m	740 m	720 m	820 m
⃝	⃝	⃝	⃝

27 A car uses an average of 6.5 litres of fuel for every 100 km travelled.

How many litres would the car use to travel 150km?

_____ litres

28 One-eighth of the length of Joe's fishing line is 17.5 cm.

How long is the fishing line? _____ cm

29 A school has 524 students. 131 of the students are in the school hall.

Shade one bubble

The fraction of students who are in the hall is closest to

one-eighth   one-third   one-quarter   one-half

⚬   ⚬   ⚬   ⚬

30 Barry paid $1.25 for bananas.

Bananas   1 kg for $2.50

How many grams of bananas did he buy?

0.550g   450g   500g   600g

⚬   ⚬   ⚬   ⚬

31 How long is there between 11:57 a.m. and 10:05 p.m. on the same day?

⚬ 10 hours and 18 minutes

⚬ 10 hours and 8 minutes

⚬ 9 hours and 18 minutes

⚬ 9 hours and 8 minutes

32 A person's electricity bill was $320 last time. **The next bill it was $240.**

What percentage decrease is this?

20%   30%   25%   35%

⚬   ⚬   ⚬   ⚬

1   4.15, 3.75, 3.35, 2.95 …

What is the rule to continue this decimal number pattern?

⬭ increase by 0.20

⬭ decrease by 0.40

⬭ decrease by 0.35

⬭ decrease by 1.40

2   This road post shows the water depth in a flood.

Approximately how deep is the water?

⬭ 9.20 metres

⬭ 9.50 metres

⬭ 9.00 metres

⬭ 9.90 centimetres

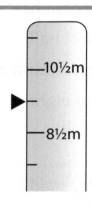

10½m

8½m

3   **Which of these has the same value as 88 × 7?**

80 × 7 + 7 + 8	80 × 7 + 8 × 7	17 × 80	80 × 7 + 12 × 8
⬭	⬭	⬭	⬭

4   **$30¼ is equal to**

$30.20	$30.25	3030 c	3075 c
⬭	⬭	⬭	⬭

5   3¼ + 4 + 6/8

_____

6   **Which has the least liquid in it?**

 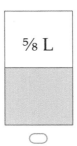 

½ L   ⅝ L   ¾ L

○   ○   ○

---

7   A number is multiplied by itself and then 27 is added. The answer is 316.

What is the number? _____

---

8   The area of this shaded rectangle is 364 cm².

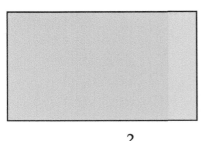

14 cm   (not to scale)

_____ ?

What is the length of the rectangle? _____ cm

---

9   Blocks make this pattern.

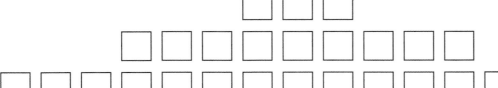

If this pattern continues, how many blocks will be in the 7th row?

45   40   50   39

○   ○   ○   ○

10 A container holds 25 red, 8 blue, 15 yellow and 12 green marbles. A person takes one marble from the container.

What is the chance that the marble is yellow?

Shade one bubble

½	⅕	³⁄₁₀	¼
○	○	○	○

11 Jan has 56 green pencils and 14 red pencils.

What fraction of the pencils is red?

½	⅕	¼	⅓
○	○	○	○

12 A rectangular paddock has a perimeter of 76 metres.

The length of the longer side is 22 metres.

What is length of the shorter side?

_____ metres.

13 **What is $6.25 as a percentage of $25?**

Shade one bubble

15%	30%	25%	20%
○	○	○	○

14 A balance shows that 10 cans have the same mass as 5 blocks.

How many blocks balance 5 blocks and 20 cans?

25	15	20	10
○	○	○	○

15 A pile of papers has 920 sheets. One-quarter

of the sheets are yellow and the rest are white.

50% of the white sheets are used.

How many sheets are used?

345	350	340	365
○	○	○	○

Shade one
bubble

16 The number of shapes in groups is shown below.

Number of groups	2	3	4	5
Number of shapes	16	24	32	40

What is the minimum number of groups needed for 160 shapes?

18	21	20	22
○	○	○	○

17 A 3D object has 2 faces. One face is circular.

The object is a

prism	cylinder	cone	sphere
○	○	○	○

18 1.25 of $16 is

$18	$19	$20	$22
○	○	○	○

© Don Robens
Coroneos Publications

Year 7 Numeracy
NAPLAN*-Format Practice Tests

19 The time difference between City A and City B
on the same day is shown below.

Shade one bubble

City A 04:15 a.m.	City B 12:05 p.m.

When it is 12:30 p.m. on Tuesday in City A, what time is it in City B?

○ 8:55 p.m. Tuesday

○ 8:55 a.m. Wednesday

○ 8:20 p.m. Tuesday

○ 8:20 p.m. Wednesday

20 Which arrow is pointing to the location of 10% of this number line?

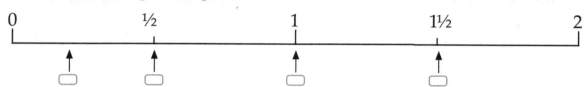

21 △ and ☐ are numbers. ☐ and △ are related by a rule.

☐	△
2	14
3	20
4	26
5	32

What is the rule?

○ △ = 5 × ☐ + 1

○ △ = 6 × ☐ + 2

○ △ = 7 × ☐ + 0

22 What fraction is halfway between ¼ and 1¼?

_____

23 The temperature of some water is 18°C.

The water temperature becomes 25°C colder.

What is temperature of the water now? _____°C

24 The dimensions of a large room are triple those of a small room. Both rooms are rectangular prisms.

The volume of the small room is 15 cubic metres.

What is the volume of the large room?

- ⬭ 400 cubic metres
- ⬭ 405 cubic metres
- ⬭ 450 cubic metres
- ⬭ 550 cubic metres

25 Which set of fractions is ordered from smallest to largest?

- ⬭ ¼, ⅜, ½, ⁷⁄₁₀
- ⬭ ½, ⅔, ¼, ⁵⁄₄
- ⬭ ⅕, ⅘, ²⁄₁₀, ⅗
- ⬭ ⅕, ⁶⁄₅, ½, 1

26 A clock shows 12 o'clock.

What is the size of the larger angle between the minute and the hour hands?

_____°

27

| 23:40 |

Shade one bubble

What analog time is the same as the above 24 hour time?

11:50 a.m.   11:40 p.m.   11:40 a.m.   11:50 p.m.

    ◯   ◯   ◯   ◯

28 Another way of writing 5^3 is

$5 + 5 + 5$ 5×3 $5 \times 5 \times 5$ 50×3

    ◯   ◯   ◯   ◯

29 17.3 km is equal to

◯ 173 m

◯ 1 730 m

◯ 17 300 m

◯ 17.73 m

30 **What is $12.50 as a percentage of $100?**

Shade one bubble

12.00%   12.55 %   12.50%   25.00%

    ◯   ◯   ◯   ◯

31 **What is the missing number?**

$20 \times \underline{\hspace{1cm}} = 16 \times 20$

32 **Which fraction has the same value as $4\frac{3}{4}$?**

$\frac{18}{4}$ $\frac{19}{4}$ $\frac{20}{4}$ $\frac{17}{4}$

    ◯   ◯   ◯   ◯

1 $\square = 15$

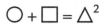 Shade one bubble

$\triangle = 7$

$\bigcirc + \square = \triangle^2$

Which number does $\bigcirc$ equal?

36	33	34	29
◯	◯	◯	◯

2   A building was completed in 1387.

In 2010, how many years ago was this?

523 years	623 years	625 years	615 years
◯	◯	◯	◯

3   A fast train travelled 973 kilometres in 7 hours.

What was the average speed in kilometres per hour?

259	139	239	249
◯	◯	◯	◯

4   Two places are 6.9 cm apart on a map.

On a map 1 cm represents 20 km.

What is the actual distance between the two places?

128 km	137 km	138.5 km	138 km
◯	◯	◯	◯

5   **Round 5 655 789 km to the nearest ten thousand kilometres.**

5 666 000	5 660 000	5 700 000	5 606 000
◯	◯	◯	◯

6

| -3 | -2 | -1 | 0 | 1 |

The arrow points to a position on the number line.

What number is at this point? _____

7 Peta thought of a number. She multiplied her number by 100 and divided it by 15. The answer is 180.

What is the number? _____

8 There are 3 properties for sale.

Which is the *smallest* property?

85 m / 25 m

35 m / 70 m

45 m / 50 m

○   ○   ○

9 A swimming pool has a capacity of 28.50 kilolitres.

How many litres does the swimming pool hold when it is full?

28 500   2 850   2 805.50   285.00

○   ○   ○   ○

10 16.94 + 7.49 = _____ + 4.77

11 Alex bought 7 pens (all the same price) and a $31 book. They cost $94.

What do 5 pens and a $23 book cost?

$65 $68.50 $68 $71.50

○   ○   ○   ○

12 $76 \times$ _____ $= 19$

What is the value of _____?

2/3	½	1/3	¼
○	○	○	○

Shade one bubble

13 George bought a camera. Its price was 35% less than its original price.

The original price was $750.

What did he pay for the camera?

$ 488	$262.50	$487.50	$387.50
○	○	○	○

14 A book has 105 pages.

35 pages had illustrations.

What fraction of the book is illustrated?

½	¼	⅓	⅔
○	○	○	○

15 A person sets their watch and alarm clock to different times.

Watch	06:55 (a.m.)
Alarm clock	**35 past 7 o'clock (a.m.)**

When the alarm clock shows 10 past 12 o'clock (p.m.) what time will their watch show?

11:25 a.m.	11:40 a.m.	11:30 a.m.	12:20 p.m.
○	○	○	○

16 The time is 21:55.

What time will it be in 39 minutes?

_____ : _____

---

17 The height of one book is about 6 cm.

About how high would 680 books be in centimetres?

Shade one bubble

| 4 180 | 4 080 | 4 079 | 4 084 |
| ○ | ○ | ○ | ○ |

---

18 This calculation gives the average speed (kilometres per hour) of a space craft over a short time interval.

$$\frac{45.765 - 9.684}{3.06}$$

What is the average speed of the space craft?

_____ kilometres per hour

---

19 The mean (average) of six numbers is 67.

A seventh number is added and the mean becomes 78.

The number that was added was

| 143 | 145 | 144 | 244 |
| ○ | ○ | ○ | ○ |

---

20 A person used identical cubes to build a rectangular prism.

There were 16 cubes in its base.

128 cubes were used altogether.

Which of these could be the dimensions of the prism?

| $4 \times 4 \times 4$ | $8 \times 2 \times 8$ | $8 \times 2 \times 12$ | $8 \times 1 \times 8$ |
| ○ | ○ | ○ | ○ |

---

21 A car dealer has 7 times as many new cars as used cars.

Altogether there are 608 cars.

How many new cars are there? _____

22 Which of these is in ascending order?

Shade one bubble

○ 0.03, 0.003, 0.33, 0.0003

○ 0.008, 0.08, 0.80, 8.80

○ 0.002, 0.52, 0.2, 0.22

○ 3.1, 3.01, 3.001, 30.1

23 A pyramid has a square base.

The area of the square base is 324 m².

What is the length of one side of the base? _____ m

24 Which number is five thousand and nine?

Shade one bubble

5 009	5 090	5 900	5 900
○	○	○	○

25 Which number is exactly halfway between 1.6 and 2.8?

2.5	2.3	2.2	2.3
○	○	○	○

26 Tim ran for 2½ minutes. He ran at a speed of 4 metres a second.

How far did he go?

650 m	700 m	600 m	620 m
○	○	○	○

27 A car uses an average of 8.5 litres of fuel for every 100 km travelled.

How many litres would the car use to travel 250 km?

_____ litres

28 One-sixth of the length of a fishing line is 26.5 cm.

How long is the fishing line? _____ cm

29 A school has 520 students.

65 of the students are in the school hall.

Shade one bubble

The fraction of students who are in the hall is closest to

one-eighth   one-third   one-quarter   one-half

○   ○   ○   ○

30 Elizabeth paid $1.50 for bananas.

Bananas   1 kg for $2.00

How many grams of bananas did she buy?

0.750g   750g   700g   650g

○   ○   ○   ○

31 How long is there between 07:57 a.m. and 09:05 p.m. on the same day?

○ 1 hour and 18 minutes

○ 1 hour and 8 minutes

○ 1 hour and 28 minutes

○ 1 hour and 4 minutes

32 A person's electricity bill was $360 last time. The next bill was $270.

What percentage decrease is this?

20%   30%   25%   35%

○   ○   ○   ○

1   4.25, 3.55, 2.85 …

Shade one bubble

What is the rule to continue this decimal number pattern?

○ increase by 0.90

○ decrease by 0.60

○ decrease by 0.70

○ decrease by 1.50

2   This road post shows the water depth in a flood.

Approximately how deep is the water?

○ 11.20 metres

○ 10.50 metres

○ 11.00 metres

○ 10.90 centimetres

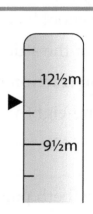

3   **Which of these has the same value as 98 × 60?**

90 × 6 + 8 × 0   90 × 60 + 8 × 60   65 × 98   90 × 60 + 8 + 60

○   ○   ○   ○

4   **$99¾ is equal to**

$99.34 $99.55   9 975 c $997.50

○   ○   ○   ○

5 $4¾ + 7 + ⅞ =$ _____

6   **Which has the *least* liquid in it?**

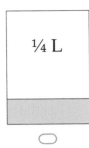

¼ L   ⅜ L   ⅓ L

○   ○   ○

7   A number is multiplied by itself and then 48 is added. The answer is 129.

What is the number? _____

8   The area of this shaded rectangle is 208 cm².

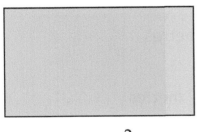

16 cm   (not to scale)

_____ ?

What is the length of the rectangle? _____ cm

9   A pattern has been made with blocks.

If this pattern continues, how many blocks will be in the 8th row?

43   44   48   42

○   ○   ○   ○

© Don Robens
Coroneos Publications

Year 7 Numeracy
NAPLAN*-Format Practice Tests

10 A container holds 32 red, 9 blue, 17 yellow and 14 green marbles.

A person takes one marble from the container.

What is the chance that the marble is blue?

Shade one bubble

½	⅙	⅛	¼
○	○	○	○

11 Jan has 48 green pencils and 24 red pencils.

What fraction of the pencils is red?

½	⅕	⅓	¼
○	○	○	○

12 A rectangular paddock has a perimeter of 92 metres.

The length of the longer side is 38 metres.

What is length of the shorter side? _____ metres.

13 **What is $9.50 as a percentage of $38?**

15%	30%	25%	20%
○	○	○	○

14 A balance shows that 15 cans have the same mass as 5 blocks.

How many blocks balance 8 blocks and 15 cans?

12	11	15	13
○	○	○	○

15 A pile of papers has 680 sheets.

One-quarter of the sheets are yellow and the rest are white.

50% of the white sheets are used.

How many sheets are used?

Shade one bubble

245	250	255	265
◯	◯	◯	◯

16 The number of shapes in groups is shown below.

Number of groups	2	3	4	5
Number of shapes	22	44	66	88

What is the minimum number of groups needed for 176 shapes?

8	9	10	12
◯	◯	◯	◯

17 A 3D object has 3 faces, 0 vertices and 2 edges.

The object is a

prism	cylinder	cone	sphere
◯	◯	◯	◯

18 0.125 of $16 is

$3	$1.50	$2.50	$2
◯	◯	◯	◯

19 The time difference between City A and City B on the same day is shown below.

| City A   08:35 a.m. | City B   14:05 p.m. |

When it is 11:45 p.m. on Thursday in City A, what time is it in City B?

○ 8:15 p.m. Friday

○ 5:15 a.m. Friday

○ 8:15 a.m. Friday

○ 7:15 a.m. Thursday

20 Which arrow is pointing to the location of 30% of this number line?

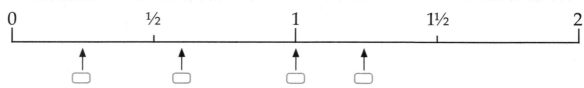

21 △ and □ are numbers. □ and △ are related by a rule.

□	△
2	17
3	25.5
4	34
5	42.5

What is the rule?

○ △ = 8.5 × □

○ △ = 8 × □ + 2

○ △ = 8.5 × □ + 10

22 What fraction is halfway between 1/3 and 1?

_____

23 The temperature of some water is 19°C.

The water temperature becomes 30°C colder.

What is temperature of the water now? _____°C

24 The dimensions of a large room are triple those of a small room. Both rooms are rectangular prisms. The volume of the small room is 9 cubic metres.

Shade one bubble

What is the volume of the large room?

- ○ 342 cubic metres
- ○ 243 cubic metres
- ○ 253 cubic metres
- ○ 234 cubic metres

25 Which set of fractions is ordered from smallest to largest?

- ○ ¼, ⅜, ¹⁄₁₀, ⁵⁄₁₀
- ○ ½, ⅓, ¼, ⅛
- ○ ¼, ⅓, ½, ¾
- ○ ⅕, ⁶⁄₅, ½, 1

26 A clock shows 7 o'clock.

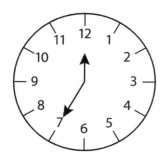

What is the size of the larger angle between the minute and the hour hands?

_____ °

27

| 21:55 |

What analog time is the same as the above 24 hour time?

9:55 a.m.   9:45 p.m.   9:45 a.m.   9:55 p.m.

○   ○   ○   ○

28 Another way of writing 3^3 is

3 + 3 + 3   3 × 3 × 3   3 × 6   6 × 3

○   ○   ○   ○

29 102.9 km is equal to

○ 1 029 m

○ 10 290 m

○ 102 900 m

○ 109.2 m

30 **What is $6.25 as a percentage of $100?**

Shade one bubble

    6.00%   6.25 %   6.50%   12.50%

    ◯   ◯   ◯   ◯

31 **What is the missing number?**

$27 \times \underline{\hspace{1cm}} = 16 \times 54$

32 **Which fraction has the same value as $6\frac{3}{4}$?**

    $\frac{28}{4}$ $\frac{27}{4}$ $\frac{30}{4}$ $\frac{17}{4}$

    ◯   ◯   ◯   ◯

1   □ = 36

△ = 10

○ + □ = △²

Which number does ○ equal?

Shade one bubble

64   67   58   59
○   ○   ○   ○

---

2   A building was completed in 1069.

In 2010 how many years ago was this?

891 years   941 years   945 years   881 years
○   ○   ○   ○

---

3   A fast train travelled 984 kilometres in 6 hours.

What was the average speed in kilometres per hour?

166   264   164   246
○   ○   ○   ○

---

4   Two places are 9.9 cm apart on a map.

On a map 1 cm represents 15 km.

What is the actual distance between the two places?

148 km   138.5 km   148.5 km   158 km
○   ○   ○   ○

---

5   **Round 2 955 239 km to the nearest hundred thousand kilometres.**

2 965 000   3 000 000   2 900 000   2 999 000
○   ○   ○   ○

6

-3	-2	-1	0	1

The arrow points to a position on the number line.

What number is at this point? _____

---

7   Jenny thought of a number.

She multiplied her number by 1000 and divided it by 25.

The answer is 1 000.

What is the number? _____

---

8   There are 3 properties for sale.

Which is the *smallest* property?

Shade one bubble

45 m
35 m
○

25 m
55 m
○

30 m
50 m
○

---

9   A swimming pool has a capacity of 56.50 kilolitres.

How many litres does the swimming pool hold when it is full?

56.500	5 650	56 500	565.00
○	○	○	○

---

10   14.94 + 9.48 = _____ + 8.73

---

11   Alex bought 6 pens (all the same price) and a $29 book.

They cost $101.

What do 8 pens and a $38 book cost?

$144	$134	$134.50	$140.50
○	○	○	○

12 69 × _____ = 23

What is the value of _____?

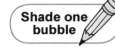

Shade one bubble

⅔   ½   ⅓   ¼

○   ○   ○   ○

---

13 Harry bought a computer. Its price was 25% less than its original price.

The original price was $1 500.

What did he pay for the computer?

$ 1 125 $1 125.50 $1 325 $1 150

○   ○   ○   ○

---

14 A book has 165 pages.

55 pages had illustrations.

What fraction of the book is illustrated?

½   ¼   ⅓   ⅔

○   ○   ○   ○

---

15 A person sets their watch and alarm clock to different times.

Watch	**07:45 (a.m.)**
Alarm clock	**05 past 8 o'clock (a.m.)**

When the alarm clock shows 10 to 12 o'clock (a.m.) what time will their watch show?

11:25 a.m.   11:15 a.m.   11:30 a.m.   11:20 p.m.

○   ○   ○   ○

16   The time is 23:05.

What time will it be in 59 minutes?

_____ : _____

17   The height of one book is about 7 cm.

About how high would 806 books be in centimetres?

Shade one bubble

5 600	5 642	5 662	5 542
⚬	⚬	⚬	⚬

18   This calculation gives the average speed (kilometres per hour) of a space craft over a short time interval.

$$\frac{37.361 - 7.609}{4.08}$$

What is the average speed of the space craft?

_____ kilometres per hour

19   The mean (average) of six numbers is 88.

A seventh number is added and the mean becomes 96.

The number that was added was

Shade one bubble

143	144	145	244
⚬	⚬	⚬	⚬

20   A person used identical cubes to build a rectangular prism.

There were 15 cubes in its base.

135 cubes were used altogether.

Which of these could be the dimensions of the prism?

5 × 4 × 9	5 × 3 × 8	5 × 3 × 9	5 × 3 + 9
⚬	⚬	⚬	⚬

21 A car dealer has 6 times as many new cars as used cars.

Altogether there are 560 cars.

How many new cars are there? _____

Shade one bubble

22 Which of these is in ascending order?

○ 0.09, 0.006, 0.53, 0.008

○ 0.002, 0.05, 0.70, 2.4

○ 0.005, 0.92, 0.5, 0.003

○ 7.1, 7.01, 7.001, 70.1

23 A pyramid has a square base.

The area of the square base is 729 m².

What is the length of one side of the base? _____ m

24 Which number is seven thousand, five hundred and one?

7 051	7 511	7 510	7 501
○	○	○	○

Shade one bubble

25 Which number is exactly halfway between 1.6 and 2.8?

2.25	2.20	2.51	2.05
○	○	○	○

26 Tom ran for 3¼ minutes. He ran at a speed of 6 metres a second.

How far did he go?

1 070 m	1 170 m	1 007 m	1 700 m
○	○	○	○

27 A car uses an average of 9.5 litres of fuel for every 100 km travelled.

How many litres would the car use to travel 50 km?

_____ litres

---

28 One-seventh of the length of a rope is 14.5 cm.

How long is the rope? _____ cm

---

29 A school has 520 students.

130 of the students are in the school hall.

Shade one bubble

The fraction of students who are in the hall is closest to

one-eighth   three-tenths   one-quarter   three-eighths

  ◯   ◯   ◯   ◯

---

30 Elizabeth paid $1.20 for bananas.

Bananas   1 kg for $2.00

How many grams of bananas did she buy?

600g   750g   700g   650g

  ◯   ◯   ◯   ◯

---

31 How long is there between 08:57 a.m. and 07:02 p.m. on the same day?

◯ 10 hours and 7 minutes

◯ 5 hours and 8 minutes

◯ 10 hours and 5 minutes

◯ 5 hours and 4 minutes

---

32 A person's electricity bill was $320 last time. The next bill it was $280.

What percentage decrease is this?

10½ %   15%   25%   12½ %

  ◯   ◯   ◯   ◯

TEST 1
NON-CALCULATOR
(pp.4 – 11)

1. increase by 0.75

2. 5.5 metres

3. $10 \times 6 + 4 \times 6$

4. quadrilateral

5.

6. ¼ L

7. 3

8. 14

9. 20

10. ⅙

11. ⅓

12. 5

13. 20%

14. 4

15. 333

16. 8

17. prism

18. 18

19. 2:30 a.m. Thursday

20. 2nd bubble

21. $\triangle = 10 \times \square - 5$

22. ¹¹⁄₁₆

23. - 13° C

24. 96 cubic metres

25. ½, ¾, ⁸⁄₁₀, ¹²⁄₁₂

26. 120°

27. 4:30 p.m.

28. 7×7

29. 7

30. 25%

31. ¹³⁄₄

32. 2.35 km

TEST 1
CALCULATOR ALLOWED
(pp.12 – 17)

1   5

2   96 years

3   45

4   18.5 km

5   9 509 000

6   – 1.5

7   14

8   150 m × 30 m

9   9 500

10 8.82

11 $8.40

12 ⅓

13 $212.50

14 ⅓

15 9:25 a.m.

16 09:13

17 2 000

18 2 243.5

19 46

20 5 × 3 × 6

21 45

22 0.004, 0.04, 0.40, 0.44

23 210 m

24 8 023

25 2

26 240 m

27 24.5 L

28 350 m

29 one-third

30 500 g

31 10 hours 53 minutes

32 25%

Shade one bubble

TEST 2
NON-CALCULATOR
(pp.18−25)

1   increase by 0.50

2   6.25 metres

3   10 × 7 + 5 × 7

4   hexagon

5.   The first angle

6   ¼ L

7   8

8   16

9   30

10   ⅑

11   ⅓

12   8

13   40%

14   8

15   123

16   8

17   pyramid

18   18

19   3:30 a.m Monday

20   1½

21   $\triangle = 6 \times \square + 0$

22   ½

23   −6° C

24   144 m³

25   ¼, ⅓, ½, ¾

26   120°

27   2:50 p.m.

28   9 × 9

29   9

30   60%

31   7

32   1⁷⁄₄

Year 7 Numeracy
NAPLAN*-Format Practice Tests

TEST 2
CALCULATOR ALLOWED
(pp.26–31)

1 17

2 83 years

3 56

4 86 km

5 7 510 000

6 – 2.5

7 35

8 45 m × 90 m

9 12 500

10 9.66

11 $39

12 1/3

13 $245

14 ¼

15 1:25 p.m.

16 08:53

17 4 200

18 648.75

19 68

20 7 × 4 × 4

21 406

22 0.007, 0.07, 0.70, 7.00

23 56

24 9 023

25 1 and ⅞

26 270 m

27 15

28 540

29 one-quarter

30 400 g

31 8 hours 13 minutes

32 25%

TEST 3
NON-CALCULATOR
(pp.32–39)

1 decrease by 0.95

2 5.00 metres

3 $20 \times 6 + 8 \times 6$

4 575 c

5

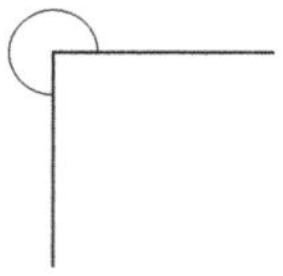

6 ¼ L

7 16

8 18 cm

9 55

10 ¹⁄₁₂

11 ⅕

12 5

13 100%

14 9

15 140

16 8

17 sphere

18 $3

19 5:50 a.m. Saturday

20 2

21 $\triangle = 7 \times \square + 0$

22 ⅝

23 - 5° C

24 270 cubic metres

25 ⅕, ⅗, ⁷⁄₁₀, ⅘

26 330°

27 7:40 p.m.

28 $7 \times 7 \times 7$

29 19 500 m

30 37.50%

31 8

32 37/4

TEST 3
CALCULATOR ALLOWED
(pp.40−45)

1   29

2   117 years

3   269

4   117 km

5   3 900 000

6   − 0.75

7   80

8   90 m × 35 m

9   19 500

10 24.29

11 $51

12 ½

13 $9 425

14 ⅔

15 1:00 p.m.

16 00:33

17 7 650

18 14.973

19 108

20 9 × 4 × 7

21 714

22 0.004, 0.04, 0.40, 4.40

23 35

24 7 202

25 2 and ⅛

26 720 m

27 9.75

28 140

29 one-quarter

30 500 g

31 10 hours 8 minutes

32 25%

TEST 4
NON-CALCULATOR
(pp.46–53)

Shade one bubble

1 decrease by 0.40

2 9.50 metres

3 $80 \times 7 + 8 \times 7$

4 $30.25

5 8

6 ½ L

7 17

8 26

9 39

10 ¼

11 ⅕

12 16

13 25%

14 15

15 345

16 20

17 cone

18 $20

19 8:20 p.m. Tuesday

20 First arrow from the left

21 $\triangle = 6 \times \square + 2$

22 ¾

23 - 7° C

24 405 cubic metres

25 ¼, ⅜, ½ , ⁷⁄₁₀

26 360°

27 11:40 p.m.

28 $5 \times 5 \times 5$

29 17 300 m

30 12.50%

31 16

32 1¾

TEST 4
CALCULATOR ALLOWED
(pp.54–59)

1	34	**23**	18
2	623 years	**24**	5 009
3	139	**25**	2.2
4	138 km	**26**	600 m
5	5 660 000	**27**	21.25
6	– 2.5	**28**	159
7	27	**29**	one-eighth
8	85 m × 25 m	**30**	750 g
9	28 500	**31**	1 hour 8 minutes
10	19.66	**32**	25%
11	$68		
12	¼		
13	$487.50		
14	⅓		
15	11:30 a.m.		
16	22:34		
17	4 080		
18	11.791		
19	144		
20	8 × 2 × 8		
21	532		
22	0.008, 0.08, 0.80, 8.80		

TEST 5
NON-CALCULATOR
(pp.60–67)

Shade one bubble

1	decrease by 0.70	**23**	- 11° C
2	11.00 metres	**24**	243 cubic metres
3	$90 \times 60 + 8 \times 60$	**25**	¼, ⅓, ½, ¾
4	9 975 c	**26**	210°
5	12	**27**	9:55 p.m.
6	¼ L	**28**	$3 \times 3 \times 3$
7	9	**29**	102 900 m
8	13	**30**	6.25%
9	44	**31**	32
10	⅛	**32**	²⁷⁄₄
11	⅓		
12	8		
13	25%		
14	13		
15	255		
16	9		
17	cylinder		
18	$2		
19	5:15 a.m. Friday		
20	Second arrow from the left		
21	$\triangle = 8.5 \times \square$		
22	⅔		

TEST 5
CALCULATOR ALLOWED
(pp.68–73)

1	64	**23**	27
2	941 years	**24**	7 501
3	164	**25**	2.20
4	148.5 km	**26**	1 170 m
5	3 000 000	**27**	4.75
6	0.5	**28**	101.5
7	25	**29**	one-quarter
8	55 m × 25 m	**30**	600 g
9	56 500	**31**	10 hours 5 minutes
10	15.69	**32**	12 ½%
11	$134		
12	⅓		
13	$1 125		
14	⅓		
15	11:30 a.m.		
16	00:04		
17	5 642		
18	7.292		
19	144		
20	5 × 3 × 9		
21	480		
22	0.002, 0.05, 0.70, 2.4		